Roads to Forgotten Texas

Roads to Forgotten Texas

Photographs by Tommy LaVergne

Poems by Joyce Pounds Hardy

Texas Review Press
Huntsville, Texas

FIRST EDITION, 2004

Requests for permission to reproduce material from this work should be sent to:

Permissions
Texas Review Press
English Department
Sam Houston State University
Huntsville, TX 77341-2146

Cover photograph by Tommy LaVergne
Cover design by Paul Ruffin
Photo of Tommy and Joyce by Carol DeBender

Library of Congress Cataloging-in-Publication Data

Hardy, Joyce Pounds.
  Roads to forgotten Texas / Joyce Pounds Hardy and Tommy LaVergne.— 1st ed.
    p. cm.
  ISBN 1-881515-71-0 (alk. paper)
  1. Texas—Poetry. 2. Texas—Pictorial works. I. LaVergne, Tommy. II. Title.
  PS3608.A726R63 2004
  811'.6—dc22

                                           2004024024

Table of Contents

Foreword

When Tommy first came to me about writing poems for his photographs, I was flattered because his pictures were remarkable—a testimony to his love for Texas. Tommy had read my collection of poems, *The Reluctant Hunter*, about West Texas, and said, when he called me, "Your feelings for Texas match mine, will you collaborate on a book with me?" It was a challenge I couldn't resist.

I, too, am a native Texan, third-generation Houstonian. My love for our home state is as deep-rooted as Tommy's; and my thoughts ran rampant with his black-and-white images, coloring each one with my own memories, my own emotions, my own heart. I may be another generation, but our zeal for all things Texas transcended age.

I grew up riding in the back seat of an old Ford sedan driven by my father as our family traveled the two-lane highways and back roads of Texas from Houston to all points east, west, north, and south. Daddy always drove with his left arm out the window pointing to something important or some landmark important only to him, telling us all about it, and making sure that we learned just how special our Texas was. I thought he was the smartest man in the world.

Later, as our five children grew up, my husband, Tom, and I spent long summers in Galveston, LaPorte, the Hill Country, Wimberley, New Braunfels, Concan, and all over West Texas just as long as it was near water. Then we became avid hunters and knew every draw and oat patch around Brackettville, Uvalde, and Del Rio. After years of sitting in a deer blind for four and five hours at a time, I fell in love with the strange quiet beauty of the craggy rocks, the prickly cactus, and the stubby, intractable mesquite. Many of these memories are in the poems.

So, working on these poems was a labor of love. I shared thoughts and ideas with my late husband, John—another native Texan—who reminisced with me about the "old days" captured in the photographs. As I worked, I would read him the poems, and lucky for me he liked them. He was my greatest fan, my sweetest encourager, and my gentlest critic when my facts were wrong. I only wish that he had lived to see the book finished.

Some of these poems are his memories, his special knowledge of times-past, some are all mine, some are all Tommy's. Most are a precious blend of three lifetimes, of parents and grandparents and families, of childhoods revisited, relived, and recorded for posterity. My words, I hope, are a thought-provoking tribute to Texas, to its history and its heritage, to places in the heart that need to be remembered. —Joyce Pounds Hardy

Roads to Forgotten Texas

How does one describe Texas? It's a task that writers and artists began struggling with even before the Texas Revolution defined the state with a violent and inspiring birth, an unmistakable outline, and a flag bearing a lone star. I'm certainly not the first to hunt Texas with a camera—or the last—but no matter. Something calls to me along the back roads and small towns that the super highways have so sadly bypassed.

I'm not sure what it is, but I do know that those back roads and small towns have always given me a sense of comfort and relaxation. It's the getaway, I suppose. There's something about being able drive away from the city, leaving the daily rush behind and having nowhere to go but anywhere you want. This is what keeps me sane. My wife and two children have been enormously helpful throughout much of this effort, sharing my love of map reading and the excitement and anticipation of what exists beyond the next back road curve. I sometimes believe my kids aren't even aware that there are major highways leading to Dallas or San Antonio. I don't think I could have accomplished the collection you hold in your hands without my family's love and support.

I also have to acknowledge the influence of Texas historian Ray Miller and his program *The Eyes of Texas*. I once showed him some of the early images contained in this book, and he encouraged me to continue, expressing his belief in the importance of a project like this. Too often people consider the grand homes and building of our cities to be the backbone of Texas, he remarked, but that wasn't really true. Texas isn't about grand homes and buildings. It's about the descendants of those who followed Stephen F. Austin in search of free land that quickly proved to be anything but free. It's about the farmers and ranchers and oilfield workers who took the raw material of Texas and made it into something great.

And, of course, it goes without saying how thankful I am to Joyce Pounds Hardy. Her ability to turn so many of my stories, as well as her own, into poetry is a tremendous talent. She has endured many hardships along the way but somehow kept on writing. Thank goodness baseball season doesn't last all year—neither writing nor pain can keep her away from her beloved Rice Owls.

The greatest influence I've had in creating these images, though, is the time I spent with my grandparents and cousins in the tiny town of Hubbard, located dead-center between Waco and Corsicana. My grandfather, John Bounds, was a barber there for more than sixty years, and Uncle Ray had a small grocery store next to the barbershop. There I could get all the treats I wanted as long as my grandmother didn't know.

The barbershop had two chairs: one for customers and one for grandkids. We'd play in that chair for hours, spinning around making each other dizzy and releasing the back so we could lie down for that make-believe shave. Both walls were lined with mirrors, and our reflections went on forever. I remember trying so hard to see the end of those reflections.

The real fun for me came after the shop closed or on Sundays when my grandfather was home. "Let's go for a ride, Paw-Paw," I'd beg. "Where you want to go?" he'd ask, knowing full well my response: "Down a dirt road!"

And off we'd ride down some old byway, over red rock hills, across one-lane wooden bridges, and past fields of corn and cotton. Maybe there'd be an old homestead, paint peeled by the sun and looking haunted, or an old barn with loose tin banging in the summer wind. There was the cemetery where Paw-Paw's parents and old friends rested, and we'd stop, read the dates, pull weeds, and water the flowers simply out of respect.

Paw-Paw told me about everything from insects to Indians. Why bluebonnets are thicker and more colorful on clay hills. Why one should check the barometer before fishing. Why you see lightning in the east and never get a drop of rain. He showed me the art of grafting a pecan tree in order to insure a better nut. Never kill a horned toad and always kill a crow. Always leave a gate the way you found it. I didn't always get the answers I hoped for. Just once I wanted to hear that a gunfighter or train robber—John Wesley Hardin or Billy the Kid—used to live in that old house. But Bonnie and Clyde were probably the only famous outlaws ever to visit those parts, and they'd just passed through.

It's funny how things sometimes turn out. Recently, on the streets of El Paso, a man stopped me and asked what I was photographing and why. I explained about this project, and he was attentive and interested. Normally I enjoy speaking to strangers, but the day was quickly disappearing, and there was one more building that intrigued me. I politely tried to excuse myself but he stopped me and pointed to the very building I was headed for. "You should photograph that," he said. When I asked him why, he looked me in the eyes and exclaimed, "That's where John Wesley Hardin was shot in the back!"

At first I got a chill, then I just had to smile. Paw-Paw, you've been with me on this entire ride. I hope you've enjoyed it as much as I have. For all those Sunday drives around Hubbard, I dedicate these images to you. —Tommy LaVergne

Roads to Forgotten Texas

WONDERLUST

You have to feel you've missed something,
to realize there's more to life
than tangibles and destinations,
more than clocks and time lines,
more than WalMart and McDonald's.
You have to feel it in your bones
—enough to leave the Interstate
and crunch down roads of oyster shell,
past marshy, brackish backwaters,
bayous and low lagoons that mother shrimp and crab,
past shanties of the fishermen
who live and die tethered to bait camps,
salty as their catch and wild
as any game they trap and sell.

You have to dare to detour, leave
the mindless miles on maps to those
who focus on the journey's end
and close their minds to new and unexpected turns.
If only once, take time to wonder
what's beyond the dogwood and palmetto,
what's beyond the tallow and the pine;
dare to wander down some road
without a name, without a number,
let the wonder of your wandering take wing.

BOSQUE COUNTY

WINDSIGNS

Small sign of life:
the windmill breathes,
in contrast
to the fallen fence,
the wild-high weeds,
the eerie hull of an empty house.
Turned slowly
by the sun-hot winds,
it pumps
whatever ghostly essence
runs beneath
its creaking heart
and stands its faithful watch
like the Queen's own guard
on sturdy legs.

GONZALES COUNTY

SIDETRACKED

If you listen you can hear it,
low and mournful, far away—the train-
like some lost child crying for Mama in the night
and Mama gone down faster tracks to see the city lights.

You can feel the quiet emptiness now boarded up inside
a hundred little stations in a hundred little towns,
bypassed by smart computers without faces, without hearts,
that leave these backroad dots on Texas maps
and precious few old-timers reminiscing glory days:
slow-moving freights and cattle cars,
hobos and red cabooses,
wooden platforms full of bustling passengers,
and wide-eyed children waving to the engineers.

If you listen you can hear it,
low and mournful as it goes—a way of life-
a time, a place, withering on forgotten, rusty vines
and all too soon only a footnote in the history books.

ROBERTSON COUNTY

SPRING-FED

What you never forget is the icy coldness of it
that cramps your toes and numbs your bones
with shockwaves when you finally jump in—
the sudden intake of breath whistling through your teeth,
the slow exhalation through shivering lips 'til the shock subsides.
But mostly, you never forget that rush of bravado that still makes you smile,
just as it did when you were a kid
and being brave enough to jump in that river
was the only proof of courage life required.

Now, standing alone in the shallows
—your holey tennis shoes keeping soft-city feet from the sharp-edged rocks—
you remember the patched innertubes that carried you over the rapids,
the hot Texas sun that baked your bare head while your buttocks froze,
the slow eddies that swirled you in the shade of a water-logged oak,
the rugged cliffs that you and your brothers dove from into Jacob's Well,
the picnic table in the middle of the river where Mama spread lunch,
the hammock between the cypresses where Daddy read his books,
the bar of soap on a string when a bath was inevitable,
the pungent smell of thick green moss and reeds edging the bank,
the feel of a knotted rope in your hands as you swung out and dropped in,
the happiness you took for granted with family around you.

So many feelings flood your thoughts,
so many scenes come alive,
the sounds of laughter still ring in your ears,
the love of it all still warms your heart.
You know now, for sure, that the river will never grow old
nor will the child who summers-on in your memories.

LAVACA COUNTY

GOD'S HOUSE

God is still here—in His church-
sitting with the ghosts of His people,
kneeling at His altar rail,
serving of Himself at communion,
chanting His Mass to the masses
though the candles have gone out
and the cross is weathered,
and hymns no longer echo inside the peeling walls.
Dust motes float in slanting sunshine
as field mice scurry through splintered pews
and unrepentant spiders spin their merciless webs.
Should God toll the bell in the belfry again
to call His people home,
would only the roosting pigeons hear?

And being pigeons, they would quickly fly away
—but always, they return—
as for the people, who knows?

WHARTON COUNTY

THE FILLING STATION

It could have been Smitty's
or Adamciks or Beegleys,
any one of a thousand filling stations
you remember on yesterday's roads
—those necessary stops for weary travelers
needing to air out the kids
or fill up the car or fix it—
usually run by a Mom and a Pop.
One at the gas pump or in the bay,
happy to talk about roads or weather.
The other inside at a cluttered desk,
working the cash register,
selling jaw breakers or Baby Ruths,
collecting nickels for ice cold sodas.

Remember squirming in the backseat,
warting your folks until they prayed
for that blessed oasis to be around the next turn?
Remember the excitement of seeing that
Union76 or Gulf or Humble sign on the horizon,
of rolling up to the gas pump,
bailing out, stretching your legs,
running the dog, lining up for the restroom,
begging pennies for the gumball machine,
sucking on that big frosty bottle
of NuGrape or Orange Crush or Big Red
or your personal favorite Chocolate Nehi
dug out of a sheet metal cooler under the overhang?
Remember reluctantly squeezing back in the car,
waving goodbye, heading on down the road,
already looking for the next one?

LIBERTY—LIBERTY COUNTY

HARD LAND

Look around and weep-
not for the dead but for the living
who had to bury loved ones here
underneath these broken rocks and rustic crosses,
whipped by wind and scorched by sun
until their names faded and disappeared
like those who left them buried in this barren place
without the promise of return,
without the hope of rain,
with only the sweetness of purpling sage
to soften eternity.

TERLINGUA–BREWSTER COUNTY

ISLAND LADIES

When stormy winds blow inland
with great gusts of gods-gone-mad,
the cottages of Galveston
just seem to raise their latticed skirts
like the grand old ladies that they are,
accepting salt-soaked feet and flaking paint
with practiced grace.

These islanders have held their own
against rapacious forces,
learning how to bend not break,
to cope with change,
to age with fading charm.
Pretty they are not nor young,
but strong of beam with solid longleaf hearts,
they struggle for gentility
and pray for soft, sweet currents in the Gulf.

GALVESTON–GALVESTON COUNTY

FLASHBACKS

The marquee says it all:
no lights, no names, no coming attractions
liven the corner of Main and Fourth
—nor have they for all these years
since the town began to drift away,
since the young folks left for the city
and old folks found T.V.,
and the box office lines grew shorter and shorter
and died.

You wanted to find nothing changed,
nothing dead, nothing gone
in this world where you grew up,
in this world where dreams once flickered
and flashed on the giant silver screen,
where hopes were born on Saturday nights,
where the you you were
became the you you are
and so you, too, moved on.

The sun still shines on the Lyric,
still bakes the painted bricks
in a mammoth kiln of summer heat,
but you feel only a rush of cool
in the shadow of its doors
and remember well the youthful heart
awakening inside.

FLATONIA—FAYETTE COUNTY

THE ROAD BACK

Tough grass lives on between the ruts
and runs like a stubborn artery
from house to barn to town and back
—should the born-here dare come back
in search of something you can't name.

Brave thing to walk the narrow scars
that time cut deep across the land
when it was green and you were young,
for now the voices are gone
and only memories remind you of what was.

COLORADO COUNTY

THE DRUG STORE

Every small town had one,
like a talisman folks had to touch
for luck, for love, for living every day
or life would lose a beat. The drug store
was its heart, the center of its small world,
pumping blood into humdrum routines,
mingling young and old with different needs,
with different passions, different dreams.
And you were there beside those leather stools,
the counter higher than your head,
when Daddy had to lift you up
to sit beside him Saturdays;
then later when your gangly legs
propelled you round and round—
kids being kids, competing for some non-existent prize.
And you were there to buy your first girl
cherry cokes or ice cream sodas,
sipping shyly, slowly through those blue-striped paper straws
until your red stool quivered like an arrow to its mark.
And you were there when Mama sent you, mercy quick,
for medicine back in the back
where antiseptic smells would make you squirm.
And you were there through all your growing up,
through all the laughter, all the tears,
through all the conversations and camaraderie of friends
— those cherished echoes lost now without walls.

GAUSE—MILAM COUNTY

THE TOURIST COURT

Somewhere deep in your childhood,
brimming as it was with mysteries
of painted braves around a tribal fire,
war-dancing for the gods, for black-eyed maidens
called by names as lyrical as yours was plain.

You felt their spirit, full of wonder, full of pride,
you felt the heat, you felt the beating of their drums
each time your folks stopped at those concrete teepees
with their scant amenities—an odd but welcome sight
along that lonely stretch of road.

No matter that the world would pass them by someday,
and weeds would grow and times would change
this almost sacred place where you had dreamed,
where even now—for you—
the campfire's ashes are still warm.

WHARTON—WHARTON COUNTY

DERELICT

Who left you mired in the mud in a slip
in the harbor of the Orange Yacht Club?
It's hard to imagine a skipper leaving you
to such an ignominious death in a rich man's
backyard. Sunk by what? A hurricane,
piracy, sabotage, lightning, neglect?
Certainly not war here in the heart of America.

No one remembers what happened to you,
to the tall, proud, two-mast yacht
that sailed into Adam's Bayou and never sailed out.
Even at high tide you couldn't float now.
You are doomed forever, it seems, just to be.
Strangers see you as an oddity,
townfolk don't see you at all.

ORANGE COUNTY

KING COTTON

The fields are brown with rows of stubble,
dotted everywhere with bits of snowy fluff
like cotton tails the rabbits left behind,
stripped clean by steel that snatches
pregnant pods from dying stalks
and shoots them into wire-screened wagons
heading for the co-op down the road.
Familiar there the sounds of men, the roar
of great machines that separate the tuffs from hulls,
the seeds from tuffs, the downy crop
blown finally into waiting bales.

You grew up watching cotton blossom
green on Texas plains, on treeless farms,
on Colorado bottom land, horizon to horizon,
nothing broke that flat expanse
except the gray-tinned cotton gin.
Gone are pickers, dragging dusty burlap bags,
heavy with their hand-plucked cotton,
moving like a rolling wave across the South.
You close your eyes and finger soft,
cool fibers of your favorite shirt,
remembering the way things used to be—
and suddenly the man is homesick for the boy.

BRAZORIA COUNTRY

BLACK GOLD

Like a forest stripped of leaves and limbs,
the derricks rise against the streaking clouds,
their silhouettes a testament to wealth,
to industry, to pride, to all
that made a state grow tall
in spite of marshland and mosquitoes,
searching, ever searching for sweet crude
deep in the bowels of their greediness.
.

Employing many, profiting few,
polluting air and bays—no matter—
oil was and is the blood of Texas.
Monolith refineries spit fire into the midnight skies;
zillions of light bulbs, sludge pits, flares,
burn like a cityscape full lit.
The lonely pumper, bobbing like a worry bird,
moves up and down and up and down
incessantly like prices at the corner pump.

BAYTOWN—HARRIS COUNTY

DREAMS

You fell in love with the old plantation,
graceful as the Spanish moss
that swayed in the morning breeze.
Its cool verandas called to you.
Its rooms stirred your imagination.
Its soul cried out for restoration.
The artist's eye saw it white again,
green shutters, open windows, curtained,
beveled-panes in a carved-oak door,
pine-paneled walls with family portraits,
polished floors with braided rugs,
your children sliding down the banisters.
A longing for what could be touched your heart.
But hurricanes and floods and time
had not dealt gently with the place,
and the "For Sale" sign still hangs on the fence
and your dreams still dance on Cemetery Road—
albeit now with ghosts.

WALLISVILLE—CHAMBERS COUNTY

THE NEW GLADIATORS

Something seems out of place here in East Texas:
Corinthian columns, arched entryways,
intricate stonework, probably red
in its hey-day—tomato red. There is something
Romanesque about the stadium, as if
gladiators should be fighting for their lives here,
not Indians—not Fightin' Indians in a Tomato Bowl
of all places. But perhaps not so incongruous
as it seems, perhaps every Friday night in the Fall
there are gladiators battling on that hundred yards
of grass and they will fight to the finish. In the end
one victor, one loser. No doubt about that.

High school football is a matter of life or death.
Parents sacrifice their sons for the glory of the game.
The bloodier it gets the more spectators scream:
scalp 'em, beat 'em, hit 'em again, hit 'em again
harder, harder, rock 'em, sock 'em , hack 'em, sack 'em, WIN!
Competition is deadly serious—player against player,
team against team, school against school, town against town.
It's all about winning, winning is all that counts.

The stands are packed, pride is at stake.
People come in great caravans to pay homage
to the game, to football, to the home team.
Stadia lights are on all over Texas on Friday nights
and the debacle would make Nero proud—
some play, some burn, and some, like you, wonder
if Rome, in all its glory, were ever as exciting as this.

JACKSONVILLE–CHEROKEE COUNTY

SHROUD

Quiescent in the channel's eerie fog,
encased like some young bride
in a gauzy veil, the shrimp boat
lies becalmed, ghostlike, in chains;
its long lines limp on creosoted pilings
pocked with barnacles,
its moorings no more needed than
a leash on a sleeping dog.

Indeed, it sleeps on the tepid mirror of the water
much as time steeps in the stillness,
much as history keeps its secrets
quietened in the softness of the air.

Nearby, long-hidden in the swampy marshes,
hidden from the passing eye,
lie treasures of the past,
old summer homes of Texas heroes
once grand, once real,
alive only on history's faded maps,
silent and lifeless as the shrimper in its shroud.

CHAMBERS COUNTY

GRUENE LIGHT

Ghosts dance here to the Cotton-eyed Joe,
foot-stomping ghosts in swirling skirts, in faded jeans,
cowboy boots, ten gallon hats—their arms locked tight
in a laughing line as Gruene Hall rocks on Saturday night.

Your grandma stomped and her children stomped
and her grandchildren scuffed the polished floor—
and your grandpa whirled them all with a beer in his hand.
Sunshine sends an eerie aura through the empty rooms
more used to sixty watt and neon lights,
inverting images of things that used to be
if you stand too long where the longneckers are,
if you think too long about yesterday.

The fiddler's tune and the guitar's twang
carry you back and back in time
and the psychedelic juke box eats your nickels
while you lean against the bar and smile
at the stolen sign, the stolen time,
the old High Life indeed.

GRUENE—COMAL COUNTY

SOMEONE'S PARADISE LOST

Nothingness covers the flat terrain,
faded and brown as a burlap sack,
dry and crisp as a cracker, it runs
mile on mile, horizon to horizon,
without a fence to climb,
without a river to cross,
without a neighbor to ease the emptiness.
Wars fought, blood shed
for this barren place, this barren land,
the victories short-lived in history's time.

Indians roamed and owned these plains,
Mexicans came and claimed it theirs,
white men brought their families and stayed.
They built their homes of adobe,
gave their hearts and struggled to survive;
but nature took back what was hers to take:
the grass, the trees, the rain, the wind—
even the wind in the windmill
that kept their dreams alive.

YOAKUM COUNTY

RETURN TO THE RIVER

Pale green and wispy sway the cypress leaves
against the geometric angles of the trestle
like some fan dancer teasing the marbled David,
hard and cold, impervious to nature's touch,
to any softness that might sap its strength.

The river, all too quiet, laps the boney cypress knees
standing like fence posts on the water's edge—no—
more like stubborn children wading, dawn to dawn,
in moon-drawn tides, delighted by the nipping shad
that nibble on their mossy toes.

Even the boats moored at the meager dock,
somnambulant, await some spark of life:
skiers, perhaps, laughing to waken ghosts of parties past;
roughnecks, telling the same stale jokes, crammed in
the canvassed barge that ferries them to offshore rigs.

Even the train that clacks from time to time
over the wooden ties breaks only momentarily
the silence of the place and hyphenates the echoes
of the past, resounding in your ears,
as if today were yesterday again.

Too lonely on this Sunday afternoon—for most—
but not for you who love this long-lost solitude,
this near-perfect old river of your childhood,
crammed with memories and wild imaginings of Caddo braves
canoeing on the blue-silk water just like you, going home.

JEFFERSON–MARION COUNTY

PROCREATION

The plough stood there with its toe dug in—
upright, sturdy, dependable, sharp—
just as it had when grandfather tilled the land,
his garden with its rich black soil,
pungent and sweet, fresh-turned and ready
for his precious seed, still growing in
the peaks and valleys of his seasons.

HUBBARD–HILL COUNTY

PERENNIAL

It took years to go back,
years to muster the courage to return
to the summers of your childhood,
to that place in time
where all that was was beautiful and good.
Nothing had faded in the mind,
love's eye still saw the sea of blue,
the rows of blooming bulbs—
Grandfather's irises that would not die.
Exuberant and wild, they were
the color of your Texas sky
beyond the sultry sun.

Now all that was, hangs on a single hinge—
one rusty, paint-flaked, three-screw hinge
that holds the gate askew,
that keeps those days of youth from being lost.
The wood-framed house, the chicken coop,
the neat green yard, the flowers gone
whose names you never knew,
except, of course, Grandfather's irises
that push through grown-up weeds
choking your heart
to bloom again each Spring.

HUBBARD–HILL COUNTY

COMMUNITY

Bells rang, whistles blew,
businesses stopped.
Barbers, grocers, druggists,
plumbers, lawyers, bankers
headed for the alley in the center of town
where the red fire truck was parked.
Neighbors helping neighbors,
the old-fashioned way
as the volunteer firemen ran.

COOLIDGE–LIMESTONE COUNTY

THE SHOP

You remember how all of those summers were:
how Tris Speaker once sat in his barber chair,
Grandfather's old friend—forever, he said,
sending grandsons those autographed baseballs
all except you, who hadn't been born;
how you listened to stories—those endless stories
of greats like Bob Feller and Ty Cobb, or great rivalries:
the Cardinals, the Indians, the Yankees—
names and games and teams important to know;
how you listened as you spun on your favorite perch—
on the cold bottom step of the chair, legs squeezed
under footrest, feet flat on the floor
propelling you round and round and round
'til the customers gave you quarters to quit;
how the smells of the shop would hang in the air—
lathered soap and Jeris,
aftershave and talcum on a fluffy brush,
even shoe polish slapped on leather shoes;
how the taste of push-ups and candy and sodas
were sweeter because they were free, free
just for you, from Uncle Ray's store next door;
how the sounds of pumpity, pumpity, pump
meant Grandmother's car was coming down Main,
meant morning was over too soon;
how she fussed at the junk she knew you'd eaten—
those strawberry lips and chocolate chin her clues,
how she fussed at Grandfather for spoiling your lunch,
and oh, how you loved them both dearly for spoiling you.

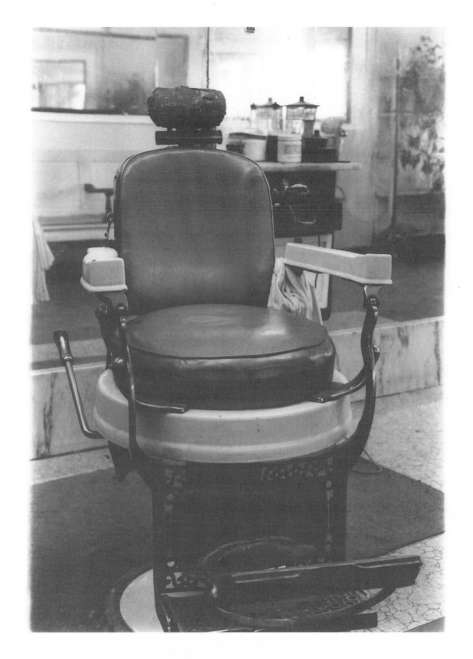

HUBBARD–HILL COUNTY

BLOCKADE

They believe the law is wrong, these shrimpers
tied together, shore to shore, across the Bay,
blocking the channel, making a statement,
hoping their actions speak louder than words,
words no one listens to anymore. Protestors,
agitators, fools—perhaps. Perhaps, just
good men hoping to be heard, desperate
for their children, their livelihood, their boats.
Truth is, T.E.D.s don't work, Turtle Exclusion Devices
keep turtles in and shrimp in or
let turtles out and shrimp out. No one is happy.
The law's a nightmare to enforce.
It's not about turtles, though the Ridley is gone.
It's not about shrimp, though the catch is shrinking,
it's all about hypocrisy—shrimp-lovers,
you can't save the turtles and eat all the shrimp you want.

GALVESTON BAY—GALVESTON COUNTY

IMMUTABLE

You recognize the road, the cedar posts,
the loading ramp, the wooly sheep,
the fence, the gate,
the cactus, the mesquite.
Comfortably the same, year after year.
Sounds of seasons are soft on your ears,
the snort of a deer, the screech of a hawk,
the cock of a gun, horses at round-up,
hooves on weathered planks of wood,
wind in the dry fall leaves.
The tire tracks are probably yours,
the old Chevy pickup's been here many times,
but maybe this is Everywhere West Texas.
Nothing's new, that's for sure.

LA SALLE COUNTY

DRIVE-IN MOVIES

An era has disappeared—
grown up in weeds,
rotted on prairies,
cracked in the sun,
displaced by TV's,
unknown to the young
who rock in plush seats
in cool cinemas
with thirty-foot screens
and wraparound sound.
Time was
when the Drive-In was
the place to be.
A dollar a car,
stuffed with friends,
a family of kids,
a couple in love,
parked side by side
on little grass hills,
windows down in summer,
up in winter,
and your very own speaker
hooked on the steering wheel.
Popcorn a dime, hotdogs fifteen,
cokes a nickel,
or bring your own.
If the kids cried, who heard?
If the couple kissed, who knew?
If the car rocked with laughter, who cared?

GARZA COUNTY

C'MON INN

Old Highway 90. Southbound.
A car-stopper, this shrimp
in its cowboy hat,
embracing the roadside sign,
knife and fork in hands,
inviting you in. Problem is,
there're no shrimp in the Brazos,
in fact, there're no shrimp
anywhere near the Brazos River,
in fact, the seafood place
that belongs to the shrimp
is no more.

RICHMOND—FT. BEND COUNTY

HAVEN

She was a lady, the Tyree Hotel,
genteel in the roughest of times,
in the roughest of ports—
Baytown between two World Wars.
Dice games rolled
and prostitutes thrived on Harbor Street.
Men flooded the area looking for jobs
—Baytown, Pelly, Goosecreek
swelled with sprawling tent cities
thrown up in promising oil fields.
Humble rushed to build dorms
for its fledgling refinery. Chaos ruled.

Lucky ones roomed at the Tyree,
well-behaved but lonely men,
far from wives and young'uns,
three meals a day,
and lunch in a sack if they asked,
two meat, one sweet, and a fruit.
Almost like home, almost.

Years have been kind to the city,
smoothed the edges of roughnecks,
made it respectable, made it grow
up and around the old Tyree,
closed now but solid still,
and like her stately palms,
tall and straight,
she casts a long shadow.

BAYTOWN—HARRIS COUNTY

COUNTRY AUCTIONS

Under a corrugated tin roof
on Thursday afternoons
in this North Texas town, rain or shine,
ranchers come
in their beat-up old pickups
and trailers of live stock to sell.
The auctioneer chants over raucous bids,
over voices that cuss and discuss cattle business—
the breeding and feeding,
lean shanks and flanks,
taxes, politicians, and the price of hay
as rapid-fire paddles snap in the air
without missing a word, without missing a beat
in this high-stakes game,
this neighborly, friendly, weekly exchange
of an awful lot of bull.

WEATHERFORD—PARKER COUNTY

LONE STAR

She watches over Texas from its Capitol Dome,
proud of the vast Lone Star she holds
—too proud sometimes of what it is,
of what it was under six flags,
an independent spirit, fighting,
always fighting to be free.
Now spread 800 miles from East to West,
near 900 from South to North,
from piney woods to mountain ranges,
sandy shores to dry flat plains—
she's big and free and feisty still
like the Texas Ranger, bronzed and locked in time,
symbolic of all of her heroes,
rugged, brave, diverse, forgotten,
those who fought and won
and wrote their names in dusty history books
hoping that what they died for
would live on.

AUSTIN–TRAVIS COUNTY

FIELD OF DREAMERS

The best thing about sandlot ball
was there weren't any adults around
handing out advice or rules or shame—
just kids filling their afternoons with fun,
teasing each other, joshing, competing
for nothing more than neighborhood bragging
that changed with every pitch. Someone
would bring the bases, someone the bat,
and, if you were lucky, someone brought a ball
that wasn't heavy with tape and hard as a rock.
In those small town days of your youth,
all the good times needed was an open field,
a backstop, sunshine, and friends.

SUGARLAND—FT. BEND COUNTY

FENCELINES

The 4x4's have weathered wind and worms,
hot Texas suns that blister men and land;
each post unique, hewn round or square,
they stand where planted by some strong,
bent back, post-holing in the rocky soil.
Barb-wired and fenced, they stretch
and corner what belonged to you,
their beauty found in rustic angles,
amateur geometry with simple laws of physics
learned not from school books but from necessity,
the ingenuity of using what's at hand, creating
maybe not what God intended
but what you invented for your gathering.
Miles from the house, a tin mail box—
holey with buck shot, red flag rusty from disuse—
points like some fat accusatory finger
toward what used to be.

Calhoun County

STAGECOACH INN

A welcome sight on the rutted road,
a rest stop for the travelers,
dusty, tired and bruised by unforgiving wheels,
wilted by heat, thirsty and hungry,
traveling from God-knows where to here,
then on to there, wherever the Butterfield Stages went.
It meant fresh horses, water, hot food,
a place to stretch your legs,
freedom from fear and boredom,
sometimes clean sheets and real bathtubs.

A marvel in its day: red brick, arches of Austin stone,
carved columns, wrought iron filigree
around its upstairs porch—
too fancy it would seem for Hackberry
but hospitality was free,
the news was fresh from the Pony Express,
and stories were told by the strangers
who shared a table on the way.
Fancy? No. Unforgettable? Yes,
say all those ghosts who still stop by
on their way from here to there.

HACKBERRY—LAVACA COUNTY

LONERS

Symbol of its Lone Star State,
the brindled Longhorn stands alone—
lean and hard, amid the thorns and thickets
of its home, its vast and rugged home
on a vast and rugged range;
an oddity of Spanish import,
rare as any in the zoo, tough and stubborn,
left to feed on cactus and salt grass
through centuries of war and wanderings,
life blood of Texas long before oil boomed,
before Longhorns and cowboys
became the stuff of legends.

LA SALLE COUNTY

MAIN STREET

Like arrows through a thousand hearts,
a thousand Main Streets pierce your Texas towns—
some luckier than others, lined with lights and life,
a shaft of asphalt running through canyons
of steel and glass, busy with businesses and commerce,
cars and busses coughing carbons in the air, and people
hurrying to be somewhere where clocks are always ticking.

Road maps color your Main Streets, red or black or blue, eight lane,
four lane, two lane, some lucky to be striped, some lucky to be paved
where once horses and wagons rolled, saloons and churches
side by side, a bakery, a drug store, feed store, blacksmith,
Mom and Pop's Emporium, a domino hall, local cafes
that specialize in chicken fried steak or Bubba's Barbeque.
They bustle in their quiet way around the county courthouse,
square and solid, built of limestone, built to stay. Still others
miss the golden ring and quiver on the edge; their destinies
a legacy of dust, old dogs and long-forgotten dreams.

FALLS COUNTY

MATURATION

Like a Van Gogh painting
the furrows draw the eye
to the sharecropper's house
to wait, to watch,
looking for shade,
for patience,
passing time
in the summer heat,
the doldrums heavy as the waiter's breath.
Long since spring rains
fresh-greened the crop
full leafed-out, lush,
enduring nature's slowness,
while the eye reflects,
waiting and watching
for red soy beans to ripen,
for these fruits of sun and rain,
of rich black earth and man's hard work
to finalize fruition.

WISE COUNTY

REUNION

The Bell Tower rests on the grassy hill
displaced by a wild tornado's fury,
a landmark oddly free of roots.
The silver hammered shingles shine
like a moon full-bright in the morning sun,
like a beacon lighting the way back home.
The bell still rings, still resonates
in ageless hearts that need no sound
to stir the lofty dreams-remembered
when the world was underneath its shiny wings.

TEHUACANA—LIMESTONE COUNTY

SATISFACTION GUARANTEED

Jesus Saves Jesus Saves Jesus Saves

You saw that once in Philadelphia,
a blinking neon sign with arrows
pointing to the tabernacle door
as if the pearly gate itself
were only open Sundays ten to twelve.

The Baytown Tabernacle has a different feel—
its art nouveau is pink and green,
muted but colorful, its message
low key without urgency
just as the timely billboard says:

"when your s'mores become a s'mess"
Jesus will satisfy.

BAYTOWN–HARRIS COUNTY

CATCH A MEMORY

You walk to the end of the old weathered pier
through shadows striping the hot planks,
remembering how they burn your bare feet,
how they burn through your bathing suit
as you and your friend dangle legs off the dock,
hoping cute boys will stop in their boats
and ask you to ski; or swimming, swimming, swimming
until hunger makes you run back up to the house.

The house is family and family is the house for you—
mothers, aunts, cousins all summer long,
sleeping on pallets, being frightened to death
by older kids who tell you hairy stories of the Lake Worth
Goat Man while someone scratches on the screen,
remembering fireworks shooting across blue water

on the Fourth of July, spraying for wasps, cleaning out
dirt daubers, working that perennial jigsaw puzzle
on grandmother's table, jigging for crappie,
fishing for fat yellow cats, making the trip to Weatherford
to the farmer's market for fresh peas, peaches, okra,
and a watermelon you can't wait to ice down,

then when breezes finally cool the evening down,
you charcoal burgers, best with those vine-ripe tomatoes.
The lake always makes you eat too much, makes you lazy,
makes the best of all lying in the hammock with a new novel
struggling to stay awake but not struggling very hard.
Now, the matriarchs are growing older and change is coming;
you walk to the end of the pier and your heart wonders
who will keep the magic of this place alive.

LAKE WORTH–TARRANT COUNTY

THE BRIDGE TO NOWHERE

A monolith, a dinosaur,
a creature from the past
who outlives usefulness
is doomed to die, and so
the girdered trestle,
once a giant,
once a feat
of engineering skills,
is orphaned
from its world
of passengers and freight trains,
of whistles and time clocks,
loved only by the
creeping vines that
hold it in their arms
and tie it to the past.

WHARTON—WHARTON COUNTY

EXHILARATION

You can feel it coming in—
the Blue Norther—with
nothing to stop that first drop
in temperature, that first
chill in the air, that first
clue that winter is roaring
across the gray-skied prairie—
one minute 99, the next 30.
Seasons are weird in Texas,
marked more by sports
than thermometer readings,
but if you're lucky,
if you're suited up
in hot pads under your football
jersey on a Friday night
when that first Blue Norther
hits, your energy sky-rockets,
your legs grow frisky,
and your mind clears as quickly
as the star-studded heaven
over the stadium
where Mama puts down her coke
and her fan, and gets out
the blanket and the hot chocolate.
Mamas always seem to know.

ROBERTSON COUNTY

CORN FIELDS

This will be a good year,
not too much rain,
not too much sun; just
one of those miracles
God sends you sometimes
when He wants you
to remember that the seeds
are His creation, not yours.

VICTORIA COUNTY

TRAINS

They still pass through our lives,
usually at rush hour when you're in a hurry
or alongside a freeway whistling warnings
to little cars that race it to the crossings.
Sometimes they clack clack clack
in the night just beyond the tallows,
—louder when the trees have lost their leaves—
and the sound always lulls you to sleep.
Always they bring back memories of running
to the tracks with Grandpaw to put pennies on rails
so the train could mash them flat, or cross
two straight pins so the train could weld them
together—swords you called them. Memories, too,
of when you and your cousin pulled all
the sticking-up-spikes out of the tracks,
put them in a wagon, and proudly
presented your gifts to Grandpaw.
He made you take them back and tell
the Station Master what you'd done.
Good Man. Hard lesson.
After that, the tracks would ripple and seem alive
—if only they still were.

DUBLIN—ERATH COUNTY

FISHING SABINE LAKE

The Orange Boat Club only has two ramps,
one small, one large, where you launch your boat
at dawn on quiet days when the lake is slick
as silk and you hate to ripple reflections.
Ancient water-logged cypress stand guard
and the gray heron watches with little interest
as the drone of your Yamaha stirs the air.
You make no wake in Adam's Bayou,
nosing the Blue Wave east toward the River,
then south toward the Lake.

With your best girl by your side, you
throttle up and head for The Pines; the
sun now reddening the horizon and
sparkling on the wind-whipped waves.
You're tempted to follow the gulls
but flounder are what you love
to challenge. Shrimp-tipped curly tails
fly on your spinning reel and
hum into the marshy grasses
to be walked along the bottom, hopefully
bobbing on the nose of some flatfish.

The troll motor eases you in and out
of coves, along the shallow banks,
into sloughs and cuts and backwaters,
past sleeping alligators and nesting birds.
There's no thrill in the world
like hooking a fighter, dipping the net deep
into green water and landing a keeper.
You're king of the hill until your best girl
catches one bigger than yours.

SABINE LAKE—ORANGE COUNTRY

ARTIFACT

Relic of the past,
without a train,
without a load of golden grain,

standing
gangly, like some giant creature
out of Star Wars,

isolated and forgotten,
waiting for Han Solo
to take charge,

to fire it up,
to find a purpose
for its being once again.

BETWEEN GLEN FLORA AND EGYPT—WHARTON COUNTY

LOLLY, LOLLY, BORDER COLLIE

Old dog gone,
under the rocks you loved
beside the ranch road going home,
your rugged, sun-tipped mountains
monument enough for you,
the collar and the cross, small tribute
for your service, loyal, tireless,
herder of sheep with a heart of gold.
Goodbye, old friend.
Goodbye.

JEFF DAVIS COUNTY

ALCHEMY

Finger of God points to a fork in the road
just over the hill, beyond the curve,
beyond the winding metaphor of life
that twists and turns—predictable
and orderly and safe—'til now

when lightning strikes and splits
your old familiar, ordinary path into a world
of choices and challenges and change.
There is no turning back once you have seen the light
and all that was can never be again.

KIMBLE COUNTY

UNLUCKY

Death hangs here on thin barbed wire,
staring out of pelvic eyes, hollow as forever
when forever is impaled upon the now,
for no tomorrow waits beyond the fence,
no green oakmott, no spring-fed stream,
no sunrise warms the small whitetail,
young and wasted on a lonely hill,
its family grieving somewhere in the dark.

KIMBLE COUNTY

REFUGE

Sometimes nature lucks out
and man improves the beauty of the place—
green water spilling over dams,
spinning on a concrete spool
that never fills and never empties,
infinity cascading into froth,
hiding you, the child again,
the dreamer who spent those sun-baked summers
tucked inside your secret tunnel
underneath the rainbow curling overhead,
its steady shush
hushing the grown-up world outside.

LLANO COUNTY

CURRENTS

What is it about a river
that makes you feel eternal,
connected to the past
and future all at once,
spawning life, nursing death?

And you in the middle
feel its power,
stand in its shallows,
wade in its eddies,
watch its passing with envy,

as it cuts a mighty swath,
wild and winding, always changing,
free of time and expectations,
always tilted downward
toward the ever-waiting sea.

EDWARDS COUNTY

LAW AND ORDER

Remnant of a small town's law,
the jail still stands in the alleyway
softened now by pink crape myrtles,
its red D'Hanis bricks still solid
on the dusty street. Sunlight blinks
through iron-barred window,
touches ghosts of bandits and fast guns,
a drunk or two sleeping it off in the cell,
a crusty sheriff keeping the peace.

Probably not much happened around these parts
but the town was ready if it did.

MEDINA COUNTY

DOUBLE DARE

The creepy aura of the haunted house
draws you slowly through the leafless trees,
the squealing gate swings at your touch,

the winter grass crackles underfoot.
You look for candles flickering in the windows,
curtains moving without any wind,.

the bottom step creaks and the porch moans,
cobwebs cling to your flannel shirt,
a yellow-eyed cat arches his back.

Your trembling hand bangs the knocker,
it sounds like a canon shot—and
heavy footsteps move to the door,

but you never see it open, you are
stumbling, screaming toward the gaping gate
as friends laugh and holler, "run, run, run"

from the safe side of the fence.

GOLIAD COUNTY

TREK

You came from Cajun country,
left your cayenne, Creole roots behind
and brought your family across the Texas line,
edging into Piney Woods,
squatting on some worn-out land,
hoping that your luck would change.

NEWTON COUNTY

CATHERINE
1825-1858

The Texas sun still bakes
the carvings on the headstone,
still bakes the slave-made bricks
that hold you in your early grave.

Your wealth no shield from death
when heaven calls,
your body mingled now with dust
that money cannot resurrect.

Plantation walls that held your laughter,
dried your tears, knew your dreams,
have crumbled like you, Catherine,
long-forgotten by a passing world.

WHARTON COUNTY

THE VERDICT

Imagine the jury sequestered here,
taken to the Courthouse Café for lunch,
oil cloth on the tables, paper napkins,
paper plates, plastic knives and forks,
a loaf of bread, cold cuts laid out on butcher paper,
mayonnaise in a jar, iced tea in jelly glasses.

Do you blame them for finding the chef guilty?

McMullen County

LEFT

One day you just quit in the far south pasture—
just stopped on a grassy hill one afternoon
and your rancher and his son walked home.
The cows no longer listen for the rumbling of your engine
or run across the field to you come feeding time,
but in the twilight of your years
you find you're grateful for the shade.

BRAZOS COUNTY

END OF AN ERA

Storms ago, wars ago, half again
a century—like stepping stones
across the vast frontier of Texas—
forts were isolated outposts,
stone and wood and gunpowder,
Cavalry and soldiers eating dust
and fighting Indians, always the Indians,
making forts a sanctuary
for the weary travelers moving West
in search of something
most of them would never find.

When the final wagon trains
rolled into history books,
and the last of the Comanche lost their war,
the West was tamed and troops went home,
leaving the forts to fight a lonely battle
against the ravages of time.

CROCKETT COUNTY

PROMISES

Remember that summer, Daddy,
a lifetime ago, when we fished for catfish,
and Charlie fried them up for us,
crispy and brown, if business was slow.

You bought me that rod and spinning reel, small,
but you said it was lucky and it was.
We dug for worms and dipped for minnows, slept
in blankets on the lumpy ground. We ate

lots of catfish and laughed and hiked and
sometimes, you held my hand when I was scared.
I thought it would go on forever—you promised—
but then, what do kids know anyway?

COKE COUNTY

PRIORITIES

You're the one who reads those historical markers,
who circles town squares reading names of stores:
Western Auto, Lerner's Dress Shoppe, Mac's Hardware,
Flo's Bakery, Smith's Fine Furniture, Elkins Drugstore, Sears.
For sure, WalMart hasn't invaded this town, yet.

You stop in Jodie's Café, the kids are hungry.
What's better than country cooking?
On the edge of town you find a "Genuine Texas Museum,"
full of rusty plows, ancient tractors, primitive combines,
stuffed jackalopes and bobcats, and the corpse of
a vintage sedan that looks like an army tank.

"Amazing," you tell your wife, "Look, kids…"
but the kids aren't looking at what you're looking,
they're busy chasing grasshoppers—thousands and
thousands of green grasshoppers hopping everywhere.

YOUNG COUNTY

THE BIG BEND

The Rio Grande bends like a bird's wing
dipping deep into Mexico and up again,
as the river encircles a strange, harsh land
of desert flats, deep canyons, and great
spikes of mountains. Scrubby plants,
cobbled arroyos, and broad barren mesas
are split like zigzags of lightning by a once-raging river,
now docile as a bird in a cage on its way to the Gulf.

BREWSTER COUNTY

INFINITY

These are not rolling hills
of soft green grass and groves of shade
or fields of wildflowers and honey bees—
in truth, a hard, unyielding land
whose only beauty lies in magnitude,
in mountains that have pushed up
from the strata of the earth
in rounded mounds
that stretch across a long blue sky.

JEFF DAVIS COUNTY

SANTA ELENA

Eons of wind and water and sand
sawed the mountains in two and carved
canyons at the bend of the Rio Grande.
The river, once deep and wide and fast,

divides Texas and Mexico—800 miles
from El Paso into the Gulf.
But nature changes and rains stop,
nothing stays the same forever.

People stole the water and fought over water
and dammed the water and polluted the water
and diverted the water
and cursed when the water was gone.

Now the border is filling with sand
and everyone walks on the river's grave.

BREWSTER COUNTY

THE LIFER

Old cowboy, you've seen all there is to see
from the back of your horse on this ranch—
the same cows, the same round-ups,
the same valleys, the same mountains,
the same sunrise and sunset year in, year out,
for as long as memory wants to remember.
Never alone, though God knows you are,
in this lonely place of endless miles and endless fences,
where tomorrow will be just like yesterday.
And that's okay with you.

JEFF DAVIS COUNTY

TORTILLA FACTORY

A business of your own—your dream
making tortillas, special light ones
with your hand-ground corn
on Madre's well-worn mortar,
far from the river where she knelt
and worked the kernels into fine white meal.

She taught you well.
Your own tortillas, rolled in balls and patted flat,
baked in old stone ovens—fresh, so fresh
the people stood in line to buy them hot
and fill with beans or rice for supper.

Times were good.

TERRELL COUNTY

HIGH BRIDGE

The Pecos is persistent—
a scrappy river slicing
through six counties of West Texas,
plains and hills, mountains and deserts,
flowing southeast toward the Rio Grande.

Out of nowhere in this desert, like a steel mirage,
the Pecos Bridge, straight as an arrow
flies from one flat, windswept plain
across the canyon cradling the Pecos
to another barren, windswept plain.

An easy crossing for you, Traveler,
in your air-conditioned car
without a thought of pioneers, Conquistadors,
lone wanderers and Indians
who had to get their feet wet fording here.

VAL VERDE COUNTY

"PLAY BALL"

The roar of the crowd still echoes
in these mountains—even after fifty years,
the Ball Park swells with memories
and Alpine swells with pride: the sell-out crowds,
the Minor-Leaguers playing ball—two games a day
and sometimes four because it never rained.
Ranchers, townfolk, cattle-busters, kids and parents,
teenagers who dreamed of turning pro,
all came together with one voice, one loyalty,
one team to call their own.
The stadium was modern then, stone-faced
with glass-brick walls, tall poles of lights
around the field, and a green diamond as beautiful
and rare as any precious stone to lovers of the game.

BREWSTER COUNTY

HISTORY REMEMBERS

Remember The Alamo! Remember Goliad!
but who remembers Goliad—
the massacre of Fannin and his four hundred men
three weeks after the fall of the Alamo?

And who remembers that the Texan Army,
heroes of San Jacinto, gathered the bones
of Fannin's men, carried them in procession
and buried them with honors in a military grave?

Goliad remembers. This isn't just another town
with country folks and country living,
a town square centered neatly in its heart,
struggling to survive anonymity—

no, this one has a star beside it in the Texas history books.

GOLIAD COUNTY

COMPADRES

Not so elegant, El Gavilan,
this bit of Mexico so far from home
that only comes alive when the lights go on.
Loud festive crowds, costumed and happy,
sing and dance and toss a few tequilas,
which too many of, make some patrons weep
for those they left behind.
But spirits rebound to the Mariachis,
strolling around the old cantina,
playing trumpets and guitars
as they caress the Spanish love songs,
making Señoritas smile
and old Señoras wish that they were young again.

TERRELL COUNTY

DRY HOLES

Like soldiers on a battlefield,
the pump jacks and the Christmas trees,
the tractor motors and the sheds
died fighting a holy war of need and greed,
sucking the living juices from good earth,
forgotten warriors rusting
in a thousand fields of weeds
without a prayer of proper burials.

LIMESTONE COUNTY

THE OLDEST SENTRY

The Confederacy left you behind,
left you to guard Ann Street
as you've done for a hundred and fifty years,
as you did for the old Ross home,
the Brackett News,
the crumbling remains of a lively frontier town,
full of trappers, scouts, and traders,
whores, cowboys, and just good folks
looking for a home.

Now Ann Street has sidewalks and curbs,
one stop light, and pickups instead of
wagons, horses and mules.
No more cavalry fighting Comanches
in an isolated dust bowl where
nothing would grow except angora sheep.

Today, the dust has settled
and all those wild tales you could tell
lie rusting in your heart.

KINNEY COUNTY

SELF-PRESERVATION

The quiet so quiet you can hear a twig snap,
a deer wheeze, a squirrel chitter,
a turkey gobble, a pecan fall out of a tree.
Life seems to happen by chance out here
where people are few and living is hard,
wild life scratch and claw for food,
nature survives with stickers and thorns.
But you can bet next week's paycheck
that cow, fat and sleek, walking up the loading ramp
knew exactly where the golden hay dumps were.

La Salle County

DEAD END

Why does this doorway make you think of death?
Dark and cold, a door with nothing on the other side,
forgettable as headstones with no place in history.

Not faraway, forgotten markers etched with fading names,
haunt you more than Houston's grave—
his monument impressive, brave words march across the stone
as he had marched across Texas for freedom.
This his cemetery, pay due homage to the man.

But other graves and other men, whose struggles ended in this ground
without fanfare or glory, lost in his great shadow,
lived and died so young, the women and the children,
sad, sweet stories on their headstones broke you heart.
So many fevers, fevers you have only read about in books,
invisible these enemies no army could defeat.

Ironic that Sam Houston, soldier in so many bloody battles,
lived to twice the age of those buried beside him here. Hero or not—
they all pass through the same dark door of death.

WALKER COUNTY

REST STOP

The drive was long and the kids were getting restless,
so you stopped in Schulenberg. An oompah
oompah band played waltzes and polkas
on a small grandstand in the city park
for those who loved to dance and dance
and dance and dance on the concrete floor
where the cattle auction was last week.

The beer was cold and the German sausage
cooking on the open grill had a calming effect
on your nerves. The kids danced off some energy
and you swirled your wife around a time or two.
The smell of the warm kolaches in the bag
beside your driver's seat kept a smile on your face
long after you and your family hit the road.

FAYETTE COUNTY

NO CONTEST

The land can't win against the sea,
against the Gulf's incessant appetite
for sandy shores and stilted houses
built beyond the rooted safety of the dunes.

Man is stubborn, dogged, willful,
as are floods, high tides, and storm surges
colliding on imaginary lines
that leave man hanging out to dry every time.

MATAGORDA COUNTY

SILENCE

Mr. Bishop paved wide sidewalks and wide streets,
planted 600 palm trees and named the town
for himself before he sold a single lot to comers.
Ambitious, his town grew. Twenty-eight hundred souls
prospered on cotton and grain and Longhorns.
Then the Depression came.

The passage of time has not been kind to Bishop.
The town is deserted—not vandalized, not burned,
not destroyed—just closed down for a long while.
Huge nameless trees grow out of the bowels of the buildings,
a few palm trees are scattered here and there,
no glass is broken, no graffiti scars the yellow bricks—
not even a ghost survived to tell what happened or when or why.

NUECES COUNTY

DELUGE

Not your typical day in South Texas.
Not what you hoped to see
on the first day of Fall—
no lush winter greens
in flawless rows of fertile soil,
no citrus trees heavy with golden fruit.

The rains are relentless,
flood-minded,
drowning highways and ranch roads.
The tail end of a tropical storm
fills furrows and ditches and streams
that are more used to drought and dust
and irrigation.

Someone overdid the rain dance.

WILLACY COUNTY

ENOUGH

Life is not always sunshine,
blue skies and golden bales of hay.
Even the cows in this butter country
get tired of the rain when it rains
and rains and rains and rains
and they have to walk home
in the knee-deep water,
hungry and probably mad
with the bell-cow leading the way.

KENEDY COUNTY

QUE PASA?

Mystery shrouds the building—
its story lost,
its history more than just a shop,
just an office, just another restaurant.

Someone's dreams are standing here,
gutted, naked, forgotten.
The bearded palms can count seventy years,
more or less, just twigs when adobe
first covered the bricks like skin
stretched too tight over wooden bones.

Aztec mosaics outline the door,
thunderbirds guard the entry.
Above the windows a faded mural
—people and wings and feathers—
survive the ravages of time
and mourn the loss
of life and laughter and tomorrows.

WILLACY COUNTY

OUTMODED

The old bank probably died of a heart attack
when modern banking soared into cyberspace.

Old-fashioned and empty it stands,
solid but severed from today's world
of high finance, computerized accounts,
electronic transactions, e-mail, dot com's,
blinking screens, online, web pages,
drive-thru windows, ATMs, PINs, credit cards,
debit cards, passwords, recorded voices:
press one for English, two for Spanish,
canned music while you wait and wait,
customers who are just numbers on a check.

The old banker who built the bank on a handshake
would not like the changes.

KLEBERG COUNTY

DESTINATION TEXAS

Canada geese fly south in perfect formation
to winter in Gulf Coast marshes,
feast in rice fields,
mix with other migratory flocks.
Pickings are good, the air warm and humid,
the water sweet and cool.

Come Spring, parents gather their young
and teach them the rest of the ancient route
back home to ancestral breeding grounds
on northern lakes and prairies.
They fly thousands of miles for a few months
of sunshine—much like you and me.

.

DALLAM COUNTY

THAT'S LIFE

Nothing's more important in a cowtown
than a depot for shipping cows.
The train keeps Hereford, the town, alive—
population 15,885, but not
the three million doomed Herefords, the cows,
happily run out of town on a rail.

DEAF SMITH COUNTY

FIRST LIGHT

Dawn on the High Plains
lights up the ruffled clouds
that seem to be waves rolling to shore,
but there is no water here,
no rain clouds promising rain
for this parched flat land.
Telephone poles and power lines
and this black-top road with long, white stripes
point to the horizon and promise a town
just beyond the curve of the earth.

LUBBOCK COUNTY

DESPERATE MEASURES

Startling sight on old Route 66—
embankments of upended automobiles,
shot full of holes circa Bonnie and Clyde,
vintage Cadillacs and Fords and Buicks
as far as the eye can see.

Ranchers planted cars to bank the sand
and grass to hold it down—
windbreaks to keep their land from moving,
to stop the soil from blowing away.
Odd-looking dunes on the open range.

Oldham County

WINTER JEWELS

December
freezes the Canadian River's own froth
into icy drifts and floes
that swirl like scattered stars in an inky sky.

Blasts of Arctic winds
blow through thin barbed wire fence
leaving a frozen necklace around
the long, fair neck of the Panhandle.

OLDHAM COUNTY

WHAT'S IN A NAME?

Beef jerky, pork jerky,
lamb jerky, goat jerky,
all of it tastes the same
and maybe it is.

If a rose is a rose is a rose,
then jerky can be jerky can be jerky,
who knows?

LAMB COUNTY

HERITAGE

Only church in the county—Saint Maria,
a masterpiece of German craftsmen,
rock-solid, reassuring, a massive presence
in this Catholic dairy-farming community
of 440 souls .

Candles flicker in the Old World Grotto,
their smoke carrying prayers to Heaven
as they have for a hundred years.

Ten o'clock bells break the silence
on this quiet Sunday morning
and worshippers come out of every door
walking to church—one young girl laughing,
running to catch up with her friends.

ARCHER COUNTY

HUECO TANKS

A sacred place among the boulders and caves
of this desert crossroads, a gathering place
where hollows filled with water and sustained life,
where ancestors of Tiguans and Pueblans,
tens of thousands of years ago, carved and painted
images on the rock faces of these hills
—kachina-like masks, bug-eyed figures, red horses,
prehistoric treasures, pictographs of what?
their imaginings? their gods? their world?

EL PASO COUNTY

LA CUIDAD INTERNATIONAL

A stone's throw away from barkers and beggars in Juarez,
in a hectic border-hopping zone,
the Alamo Shooter's Supply guards its corner
as El Paso once guarded the Old West frontier.
For centuries, cultures have merged and clashed,
wedged between the Rio Grande and Franklin Mountains.
Anglos, Hispanics, and Native Americans blended
into a warm, friendly, welcoming lot,
comfortable with each other and where they are.

You can feel a difference in the people, in the hot dry air,
in the Elvis music coming from Dave's Pawn Shop across the street,
in the spicy Mexican food at Taps Bar around the corner,
in the polished museums and ornate churches,
in the eclectic montage of its neighborhoods.
There is a different flavor on this western edge of Texas,
it is a combination plate worthy of a master chef.

EL PASO COUNTY

CADDO LAKE

You hunted and fished this Red River Valley
long before the lake was formed,
before the earthquake and giant flood waters
covered your Village to punish the Chief
who ignored Great Spirit's warning
to move his people to higher ground.
Or so your Caddo Legend goes.

The only natural lake in Texas,
this sprawling maze of sloughs, bayous, and ponds.
Twenty-six thousand acres of bald cypress swamp
tangled with lily pads and American lotus,
smooth cypress knees poke up through the water,
alligators and snakes, frogs and beavers,
mink and deer, armadillo and raccoon
thrive around this placid lake
teeming with seventy-one species of fish.

An anomaly today, still primitive, pristine,
preserved, you hope,
for generations yet to be born.

MARION COUNTY

CLOSURE

There comes a peace in the evening—
a quiet that isn't really quiet at all,
leaves tapping fingers on limbs,
noses of armadillos snuffling,
tireless runs of scuffling squirrels,
soft hissing of the hidden deer,
birds talking back and forth
in that incessant twittering they do so well;
even the grass crackles and pops,
and old trees bend and groan as if
their aching joints know this day's warmth is gone,
and gates that make no sound
stretch taut across the gaps of time and space.

DEWITT COUNTY

Joyce Pounds Hardy is a graduate of Rice University, Class of '45, BA English, 1967, native Texan, writer and poet, winner of the Texas Writer's Recognition Award given by the Texas Commission On The Arts under the auspices of The Texas Institute Of Letters, a grant for publication of her first book of poetry: *The Relcutant Hunter*, Latitudes Press, 1990. The poem "Contemplation" from that book was nominated for the Pushcart Prize.

Her second book entitled *French Windows*, Eakin Press, is a collaboration of poetry with four friends from The Paris American Academy, Paris, France. Her newest publication, a narrative memoir entitled *Surviving Aunt Ruth*, 1st Books Library, came out last December.

She has had poems published in literary journals such as *Touchstone, Stone Drum, i.e. magazine, Dragonfly, Amelia, Lucidity*; magazines such as *Theater Monthly, Fan,* and *Creative Lifelines*; anthologies such as *Suddenly, Texas Poetry Calendar 2005, Houston Poetry Fest, From Hide and Horn, Poetry Society of Texas, Many-Eyed Landscape, When the Wind Stops*, a collection of Desert Storm poems, and *Poetry Online,* as well as editorials in the "Outlook" section of the *Houston Chronicle*, The *West University Examiner*, and articles in the *Rice Alumni* magazine,

SALLYPORT. She also writes a weekly football column in season for *The Rice Football Webletter*.

Three times chosen a Juried Poet of the Houston Poetry Fest and a Guest Poet in 1997. Winner of the International Civic Pegasus Award from Poetry In The Arts, Austin, Texas, and Special Guest Reader, Texas Circuit. Poetry readings at Shakespeare and Co., Val de Gras, Paris American Academy, and L "Hotel in Paris, France: Barnes and Noble, Border's, Brentano's, and Rice University Authors' Reception. She was commissioned by Rice University to write a poem commemorating the One Hundredth Anniversary of the Signing of the Charter for Rice University, read at an Official Public Ceremony in 1990, and KTRU recorded her reading of *The Reluctant Hunter* for the Fondren Tape Library.

She was recently awarded the 2003 Gold Medal by Rice University, the highest award given to alumni. She is widowed, has five married children, thirteen grandchildren, and two great-grandchildren. She lives in Houston, Texas.

Tommy LaVergne attended Texas A&M Universityand Sam Houston State University and completed an Associate Degree in Photography from the Art Institute of Houston in 1986. For the last 17 years, he has been University Photographer for Rice University.

His assignments, many of which have been for Rice, have given him the opportunity to photograph an extremely diverse group of dignitaries and educators, including five United States Presidents: Nixon, Ford, Carter, Bush, and Clinton, as well as Henry Kissinger, John Connally, James A. Baker III, Colin Powell, Vladimir Putin, Mikhail Gorbachev, Helmut Kohl, Madeleine Albright, Yassar Arafat and U.N. Secretary Kafi Annan.

His photographs have been published in *Newsweek, The Chronicle of Higher Education, Smithsonian Magazine, Texas Monthly, Texas Highways*, The *Houston Post*, The *Houston Chronicle, Exxon Travel*, and *Science Magazine*. The majority of his work appears in Rice publications and its Alumni magazine: *SALLYPORT*. He has exhibited in various galleries in the Houston area, as well as the Rice Media Center.

He was born in Baytown, Texas, 1961, and now lives in Sugar Land, Texas, with his wife, Mary Beth, son Alec, and daughter Julia.